Useful Machines

Pulleys

Chris Oxlade

Heinemann Library
Chicago, Illinois

© 2003 Heinemann Library
a division of Reed Elsevier Inc.
Chicago, Illinois

Customer Service   888–454–2279

Visit our website at www.heinemannlibrary.com

Originated by Ambassador Litho Ltd.
Printed and bound in China by South China Printing Company

07 06 05 04 03
10 9 8 7 6 5 4 3 2 1

Library of Congress Cataloging-in-Publication Data
Oxlade, Chris.
  Pulleys / Chris Oxlade.
      v. cm. -- (Useful machines)
Includes bibliographical references and index.
Contents: What is a pulley? -- What does a pulley do? -- How does a pulley work? -- Loads and efforts? -- Pulleys for lifting -- Pulleys for pulling -- Joining pulleys -- Faster and slower -- Pulleys together -- Pulleys on cranes -- Pulleys on boats -- Pulleys in machines -- Amazing pulley facts.
  ISBN 1-4034-3663-0 (lib. bdg.) -- ISBN 1-4034-3678-9 (pbk.)
  1. Pulleys--Juvenile literature. [1. Pulleys.] I. Title. II. Series.
  TJ1103.O95 2003
  621.8--dc21

                              2003003787

Acknowledgments
The author and publisher are grateful to the following for permission to reproduce copyright material:
pp. 4, 24 Neil Rabinowitz/Corbis; p. 5 Richard List/Corbis; Illustrations pp. 6, 10 Jeff Edwards; pp. 7T, 7B, 19 H. Rogers/Trip; p. 8 Imagebank; p. 9 Chris Honeywell; p. 11 Ric Ergenbright/Corbis; p. 12 Joseph Sohm/Chromosohm Inc./Corbis; p. 13 Gail Mooney/Corbis; p. 14 Jonathan Blair/Corbis; p. 15 Holt Studios; p. 16 David Lees/Corbis; p. 17 Superstock; p. 18 Stockfile; p. 20 Galen Rowell/Corbis; p. 21 Philip Gould/Corbis; pp. 22, 23 Alamy Images; p. 25 Natalie Fobes/Corbis; p. 26 Peter Morris; p. 27 Auto Express; p. 29T Kevin Fleming/Corbis; p. 29B Spectrum.

Cover photograph by Tudor Photography.

Some words are shown in bold, **like this.** You can find out what they mean by looking in the glossary.

Contents

What Is a Pulley?

A machine makes our lives easier by helping us do things. Machines are made up of **simple machines** that work together. This simple machine is called a pulley.

This woman is using a pulley to lift water from a well. It is much easier to lift the water with the pulley than with just a rope.

What Does a Pulley Do?

A pulley turns a **pull** in one direction into a pull in another direction. This worker is pulling down on the rope. The rope is pulling up on the bucket.

These curtains are opened and closed by a pulley system. Pulling down on one string makes the curtains close. Pulling on the other string makes the curtains open.

Parts of a Pulley

wheel

A pulley has two parts. One part is a wheel with a **groove.** This is called a pulley wheel. The other part is a rope or cable that fits in the groove.

groove

rope

teeth

chain

Some pulleys have chains instead of ropes or cables. The holes in the chain fit over teeth on the edge of the pulley wheel. This keeps the chain from slipping as the wheel turns.

How Does a Pulley Work?

A pulley is used to lift or move a **load.** This pulley is being used to lift a bucket. The load is the weight of the bucket that is being moved.

load

force

The **pull** a person makes on the rope is called the **force.** If the force is strong enough, it becomes bigger than the load. Then the rope starts moving.

Pulleys for Lifting

There is a pulley at the top of this flagpole. The pulley makes it easy to raise the flag. This is because you **pull** down on the rope to make the flag go up.

pulley wheel

This tow truck uses a pulley. A cable goes over the pulley and down to a hook. Workers **attach** the hook to the **vehicle.** The cable pulls the front of the vehicle off the ground.

Pulleys for Pulling

This clothesline has a pulley at each end. After the woman pins wet clothes to the clothesline, she **pulls** the empty line. This moves the wet clothes out above the street.

pulley

string

Here is another pulley that changes the direction of a pull. It is part of a **tree pruner.** When you pull down on the string, the two **blades** of the tree pruner come together.

Joining Pulleys

A loop of rope or chain can be put around two pulley wheels. When one wheel spins, the rope or chain makes the other wheel spin, too.

chain

A chain **joins** a motorcycle **engine** to the back wheel. When a pulley wheel in the engine spins, it makes the back wheel spin. This **pushes** the motorcycle along.

Faster and Slower

The pulley wheel on a bicycle's pedals is larger than the pulley wheel on the back wheel. When you **push** on the pedals, the back wheel turns faster than the pedals do.

motor

pulley wheel

belt

A **motor** turns the large **drum** inside a washing machine. The motor has a small pulley wheel and the drum has a large one. The drum turns slower than the motor does.

Pulleys Working Together

blocks

A **block and tackle** is made up of two or more pulleys working together. A rope or chain goes around all of the pulleys. When someone **pulls** the rope, the pulleys move toward each other.

A block and tackle is used to lift heavy things, such as this sunken boat. Using a block and tackle, the **force** needed is smaller than the **load.** But you have to pull the rope much farther.

Pulleys on Cranes

Cranes have many pulleys. There is a pulley at the end of this crane's **boom.** The pulley has a hook on the bottom. Cables **attach** the boat to the hook.

hook

boom

Workers are using this floating crane to build an **offshore oil rig.** The crane can lift big pieces of steel. It has a giant **block and tackle** with many pulley wheels.

Pulleys on Boats

Sailboats have pulleys for raising and **adjusting** the sails. Sailors also use pulleys to **steer** the boat. The ropes that move the sails pass through pulleys.

block and tackle

This **block and tackle** is on a huge, old sailing ship. The ship's sails are very big and heavy. The block and tackle makes it easier to lift and move them.

Pulleys in Machines

pulley wheel

Many machines have pulleys inside. This is the inside of a printer. The **print head** sprays the ink. The pulleys and belts make the print head move back and forth over the paper.

In this car **engine,** there is a belt.
It goes around many pulley wheels.
The engine turns one of the pulley
wheels. This makes the other pulley
wheels turn, too.

Amazing Pulley Facts

- The pulley is one of the oldest machines in the world. It was invented more than 2,500 years ago.
- Sailing ships were invented a long time before **engines.** Sailors lifted and moved the heavy sails by using pulleys and **blocks and tackles.**
- An elevator in a tall building has a huge block and tackle that moves the elevator car up and down.

Many cities have streetcars, such as the one pictured here. Streetcars are **pulled** along the roads by underground cables. At the central power station, huge pulley wheels keep the cables moving.

Glossary

adjust   change slightly

attach   fasten or join together

blade   narrow strip of metal with a sharp edge

block and tackle   two pulleys with a rope or chain around both of them

boom   long lifting arm on a crane

drum   part of a washing machine where you put the clothes

engine   machine that turns energy into movement

force   push or pull

groove   long, narrow hole in an object, especially for something to fit into

join   put two or more things together

load   amount of weight that you are trying to lift or move

motor machine that turns energy into movement

offshore oil rig platform used to take oil from the seabed

print head part of a printer that puts ink on the paper

pull move something closer to you

push move something away from you

simple machine machine with no moving parts

steer make a vehicle or a boat change direction

tree pruner tool for cutting high branches from the ground

vehicle machine that carries people or things from place to place

More Books to Read

Douglas, Lloyd G. *What Is a Pulley?* Danbury, Conn.: Scholastic Library Publishing, 2002.

Frost, Helen. *What Are Pulleys?* Minnetonka, Minn.: Capstone Press, 2001.

Welsbacher, Anne. *Pulleys.* Minnetonka, Minn.: Capstone Press, 2000.

Index